From Murk to
MASTERPIECE

From Murk to
MASTERPIECE:

Style for Business Writing

Geraldine Henze

Graduate School of Business
Columbia University

1984

RICHARD D. IRWIN, INC. *Homewood, Illinois 60430*

A paperbound, classroom edition of this
book is available from Richard D. Irwin, Inc.

Library of Congress Catalog Card No. 84–80444

Printed in the United States of America

2 3 4 5 6 7 8 9 0 ML 1 0 9 8 7 6 5 4

Mark and John; Mom and Dad

Preface

Caring about style means caring about both thinking clearly and communicating thoughts and information persuasively to others. Style is, therefore, particularly important to businesspeople, who write to effect changes in people and organizations. By attending to style, business writers can check the soundness of the changes they advocate as well as communicate recommended changes effectively to others.

Nothing in *From Murk to Masterpiece* is entirely new; however, it differs from other books on style in two respects. First, it focuses on style as it applies specifically to business writing. Second, it emphasizes the processes through which good styles can be achieved. Many excellent books on style have limited appeal to the writer in business because they address students and professional writers of nonfiction. In *From Murk to Masterpiece* I've tried to demonstrate how questions of style apply to business writing and why concern with style is as important to the business writer as to the undergraduate English major, the essayist, or the novelist. I've also tried to give business writers a sense of where stylistic issues fit into the overall process of composition; that is, of how to achieve good styles while composing.

Chapter 1 suggests that style is the outcome of choice. As we compose, we continually make choices about words and their arrangement; thus, we constantly inhabit the realm of style. Chapter 2 offers suggestions for living comfortably within this realm; it provides guidelines for breaking the process of composition into stages and budgeting time for each stage. It also presents a series of questions about readers that business writers should consider during the process of composition. Frequently, business writers must address recommendations for action and change to readers who have a stake in the status quo. Assessing readers' needs, biases, knowledge, and interests is usually more crucial to the businessperson than to the essayist writing for a "general" audience or the student writing for a professor.

Chapter 3 acquaints business writers with the choices they face when formulating sentences. Chapter 4 addresses organization and structure as matters of style, using the paragraph as the basic structural unit in composition. Chapter 5 extends the concept of style to the graphic communication of information.

Taken together, Chapters 3, 4, and 5 form a guide to what I think of as "systematic editing." From my experiences as an editor in the business world and a teacher of writing to MBA candidates, I've learned that certain stylistic weaknesses crop up in almost every sample of business writing. Writers can become more effective and efficient editors of their own work by becoming familiar with these weaknesses and searching for them systematically when reviewing drafts of their letters, memos, and reports. I think it is crucial, however, that these chapters be viewed as a guide to editing rather than to composing. When writers become overly concerned with whether their thoughts come out in active or passive voice, for example, their thinking gets bogged down; they begin to suffer from paralyzing self-consciousness. When ideas flow freely into words, the flow shouldn't be staunched in order to express each idea perfectly. It is better to let the words flow. One of the beauties of writing is that it allows us to return to our words and play with them until we are satisfied.

I hope *From Murk to Masterpiece* will be useful to a varied audience, including managers, students of business, and teachers of business writing. Whether used as a reference, a text, or a supplement to other texts, *From Murk to Masterpiece* should be augmented by other reading and by writing. One of the best ways to improve your writing style is to become aware of style while reading what others have written. I hope readers of *From Murk to Masterpiece* will begin to examine everything from routine memos to magazines and books with an eye for stylistic strengths and weaknesses. When you find something you're reading difficult, I hope you'll begin looking at its style. By knowing what to look for in terms of style and by becoming aware of what you like and dislike as a reader, you'll develop a good sense of what to strive for as a writer.

Nobody can become a better writer without practice, and writing never improves significantly overnight. Changing habits isn't easy, particularly writing habits. But I hope *From Murk to Masterpiece* will encourage business writers to experiment with new approaches to writing and new ways of expressing themselves. More important, I hope it will give them greater confidence in many of the strategies and tactics they already use, perhaps without even recognizing them as good approaches to writing.

Acknowledging all the intellectual and personal debts accrued in writing *From Murk to Masterpiece* would be impossible, so I'll confine myself to the major ones.

Most of all, I owe thanks to Christine Kelly, Associate Professor of Management Communication and Director of the Business Communications Program of New York University's Graduate School of Business Administration. Under her guidance, much of the material in *Murk* was first developed. Throughout the process of turning that material into a book, Chris provided encouragement and criticism, both of which contributed significantly to the final product.

A preliminary version of my manuscript was read by three colleagues in the field of management communication: Professor Robert Gieselman of the University of Illinois at Urbana, Dr. Olivia Stockard of Chase Manhattan Bank, and Ann Bohara of Wharton. The thoughtful comments of these reviewers greatly strengthened the manuscript.

On its seemingly interminable journey to final form, the manuscript was also read and critiqued by a variety of other people who made valuable contributions: Professor Charles Bastable of Columbia Business School; Gail Williams of Home Box Office, Inc.; Chris Novak of Foote, Cone, and Belding; Marcus Edward of Credit Lyonnais; Laura Hansen, who has been my teaching assistant during the past three terms at Columbia Business School, and students in my classes.

Finally, I'd like to extend special thanks to three people. Professor Irene Nichols of Northeastern University furnished support in many forms. She helped me think my way through the material on process in Chapter 2 and got me past several writer's blocks by listening patiently and intelligently to my frequent complaints of discouragement. As a non-business writer working in the business world, Lowery McClendon provided refreshing perspectives on the manuscript, which he also helped prepare for publication. Last, I am deeply indebted to Rob Rosecrans for his faith in the value of the project, his helpful criticisms, his generous donations of time and encouragement, and in other ways far too numerous and personal to recount.

Geraldine Henze

Contents

Chapter 4

Chapter 5

From Murk to
MASTERPIECE

Chapter 1

The Role of
Style in
Business
Writing

The realm of style is the realm of choice. The choices we make about clothing define our style of dress; the choices we make about spending time define our style of life. The choices we make about words in letters, memos, reports, essays, articles, and books define our style of writing.

Style includes everything not governed by rules, laws, constraints, or force. English grammar demands that we form singular possessives (in most cases) by adding an apostrophe and an *s*. To compose correct, meaningful sentences, writers must follow certain rules, like the rules governing the formation of possessives. The rules of English grammar do not tell us, however, whether to write "The company's strategic plan" or "The strategic plan of the company." When we decide between these alternatives, we enter the realm of choice—the realm of style.

Through their choices, writers reveal their motives, values, knowledge, skill, experience, self-image, and status, *whether they mean to or not*. No writer lacks style; every writer must make choices about words and their arrangement. The choices may be poor ones— uninformed, hasty, inconsistent, derivative—but they are choices, nonetheless. And they reflect the chooser— the writer—in the reader's eye. When we write, we not only reveal our choices but also record them. The relative permanence of writing (what we *say* usually vanishes even as we speak) gives style particular weight in writing, especially in business, where so much that is written remains in files, the memories of organizations.

Most of us acquire writing styles by imitation. Sometimes we consciously imitate models; at other times we unconsciously mimic the style of the writing we read. When asked to write a letter requesting payment from a client, a business writer will often search the files for letters making similar requests. In such cases, imitation is conscious, deliberate. Often, however, we imitate unconsciously, without being aware of precisely what we're imitating or why. People surrounded by poor writing usually wind up writing poorly because they imitate, consciously or unconsciously, what they read. Unfortunately, the prose written in most organizations and the prose found in many business texts provide bad models for budding business writers.

When I speak of business prose as "bad," I mean unnecessarily time-consuming to read, understand, and retain. Prose that is difficult—that makes a reader work hard—isn't always bad. In fact, rewarding prose often makes readers work hard for understanding. Reading Emerson, for example, requires concentration and persistence. A reader could spend hours, days, even years contemplating the meaning of the following passage from "Self-Reliance":

> To believe your own thought, to believe that what is true for you in your private heart is true for all men—that is genius.

This passage is difficult because it defines a complex but familiar concept—genius—in an unexpected way. It makes us stop reading to think. It invites us to recall our own experience and notions of genius in order to understand the meaning of Emerson's statement. Perhaps it makes us pause as we note the paradoxical similarity between Emerson's definition of genius and what we normally think of as "madness."

A wealth of thought and insight informs "Self-

Reliance." To discover even a portion of the truth in this essay, we must read it carefully, reread it frequently, and stop for thinking at numerous points along the way.

Compare the difficulty of the Emerson passage with the difficulty of the following sentence from a report by James Barnes, Director of Nevada's Energy Department:

> Ostensibly, the rule is being proposed to minimize proliferation concerns related to the weapons program.
>
> *New York Times,* August 16, 1983.

This sentence also requires hard work; however, the reader's work yields little by way of reward. Here we struggle to uncover a statement obscured by inflated language, buzzwords, and passive voice. We may suspect that Mr. Barnes hasn't said what he meant, and we may wonder whether the obscurity and ambiguity are intentional. Did Mr. Barnes want to talk about minimizing "proliferation concerns" or about minimizing the likelihood of proliferation? Does he mean "concerns related to the weapons program" generally, or is he referring specifically to nuclear arms?

Many good writers make us work hard, but good writers reward our labor. Bad writers also make us work hard, but the fruits of our labor aren't worth the effort. When we struggle with bad prose, we usually struggle to uncover messages buried in murk. Having taken the trouble to disinter these messages, we are often dismayed to find that they are ill-conceived and unintentionally ambiguous.

Much of the prose we find in the business world, in business texts, and in books about business is bad—

unnecessarily difficult to read—and imitation of this prose perpetuates bad writing in the business world. Bad writing has become the norm in business, a norm passed along to young businesspeople who head for the files in search of models or who unconsciously mimic the bad prose with which they are inundated.

Poor choices about words and their arrangement in sentences, paragraphs, and complete presentations result in poor prose. It is the style of business writing, nothing more or less, that makes business prose difficult to read. But if the realm of style is the realm of choice, there's hope for improvement. By understanding the options and making informed selections among them, business writers can improve both their prose and their thought.

Making choices about words and their arrangement forces us to think carefully about what we mean. When we substitute intelligent choice for mimicry in writing, we begin to discover our own meanings—what we truly think. To be concerned with style is to be concerned with thinking clearly, and expressing ideas and information well to ourselves is a prerequisite to communicating them well to others. If, as Emerson suggested, belief in our own thought is genius, then the first step toward genius is expressing our thoughts clearly and persuasively to ourselves.

Working Toward Style: The Process of Composition

Writing is hard work. When we write, we confront a myriad of choices about what to say and how to say it. What's more, each time we write, we face a different set of circumstances—different readers, different material, different constraints on our time. Therefore, no simple procedures, consistently followed, will invariably produce good prose. But many people make writing tasks unnecessarily painful by using methods of composition that guarantee both anxiety and poor results.

DIFFERENT APPROACHES FOR DIFFERENT OCCASIONS

All of us have heard some version of the maxim, "You have to think clearly to write clearly." This is true; muddy thought can't yield lucid prose. It is not true, however, that the first step in the process of writing is getting one's thoughts completely clear and organized *in one's head.* In fact, putting ideas onto paper is often the best way to discover where thought is confused. Attempts to get clear about ideas before writing succeed only when the piece to be written is short, the format standard, and the subject familiar and simple. In more complex pieces, conceptual uncertainty and ambiguity yield to clarity in increments, as writers write and discover their thoughts.

Many of us have been taught that the steps in creating good prose are roughly: (1) think, think, think until clarity emerges, (2) create a sentence outline that shows all the ideas and information the final piece will cover and the logical relationships among them, and (3) write a final draft by elaborating on each of the points in the outline. But few people actually write this way, and few writing tasks lend themselves to this approach.

The final version of a letter, memo, or report represents the results of diverse intellectual activities:

- gathering information
- selecting relevant information
- generating ideas
- discovering relationships
- recording ideas, relationships, and information
- organizing material
- communicating ideas, relationships, and information clearly, economically, and persuasively
- examining ideas and their expression critically

What's more, these activities are "messy." Although we must go through all of these steps each time we write, we usually jump back and forth from one step to another and rarely complete a step before going on to the next. For example, gathering information stimulates thought and generates ideas; the ideas we formulate direct us toward additional information and help us decide which information is relevant. Getting new information, however, may stimulate our thinking and result in new ideas. Then, as we organize material, we may discover gaps in our thinking that send us back to brainstorming in search of new relationships. Even as we compose a draft, we may think of new ideas or better patterns of organization than those we had charted for ourselves prior to writing.

The "think, outline, write" model ignores the complexity of the actual writing process. It also overlooks the fact that different kinds of writing demand different approaches. Writing a one-page letter to explain a controversial policy to the staff presents different challenges from writing a 20-page report on recent developments in the cable TV industry. Finally, the "think, outline, write" model overlooks variations among writers. An approach that works for one writer may be useless to another. Some writers swear by outlines; others swear at them. Some writers prefer to think on paper and compose numerous drafts; others prefer to do more thinking in their heads and write only one draft. Some use word processors; others dictate.

No single approach works best for every writer in every situation. Most writers in the business world must write a variety of documents, ranging from thank-you notes to technical reports. They must also write under different constraints on different occasions. Sometimes they have a relatively long time to compose a piece; at other times they must write under the pressure of a deadline. The best business writers are those who develop the flexibility to approach different writing tasks differently and who have a wide variety of techniques to call upon for overcoming problems, like blocking, that plague all writers from time to time.

ALTERNATIVE MODELS

Recently, teachers of writing, aware of the shortcomings of the "think, outline, write" model of the writing process, have suggested alternative models. Several of these alternatives are presented below, along with brief discussions of the strengths and weaknesses of each.

11

DRAFT, DRAFT, DRAFT, . . . EDIT

Many writers find that writing provokes less anxiety if they write quickly, keep writing once they've started, and view every draft as provisional. This technique is often called "directed freewriting." When freewriting, writers essentially brainstorm on paper, letting—or making—themselves write continuously on a topic for a set amount of time. When the time is up, the draft is put aside. Later, the writer returns to the draft, rereads it, throws it away, and writes another draft. Successive drafts are written and discarded until the writer produces a draft ready for polishing.

Three rules are essential to the success of this approach:

> Write continuously without concern for mechanics or style.
> Strive at each sitting to compose a complete draft.
> Stick to the time limit set for each draft.

Variations on this approach can be used when dictating. The writer can dictate thoughts into a tape recorder and either use a transcription of the tape as a first draft or listen to the tape before composing a second draft. The "Draft, Draft, Draft, . . . Edit" approach works well for short pieces that are conversational and deal with simple matters. Many people find the approach particularly helpful when writing business letters to acknowledge favors, make routine requests, or follow up on casual meetings with colleagues. These are also the occasions when many writers find dictation the most effective and efficient means of composition. In all of these situations, the writer's major goal is keeping in touch, and the message itself is relatively simple and short.

For longer, more complicated messages, writing successive complete drafts becomes time-consuming. Also, this approach tends to produce mediocre prose. It rarely generates excellent work because the writer concentrates on getting words down quickly and has a tendency to gloss over difficult passages instead of struggling to refine thoughts by finding precise expression for them. Longer pieces produced this way tend as well to be loosely organized and repetitive because the writer expresses ideas as they come to mind, instead of organizing them into a logical pattern.

DRAFT, OUTLINE, DRAFT, EDIT

This approach is a variation on the one described above. Instead of discarding the first draft, the writer uses it to identify major points and develop an outline. The second draft is then composed by following the outline and represents the final draft, which the writer edits systematically.

The "Draft, Outline, Draft, Edit" method works well for pieces of medium length (three to five pages) that cover much material and must be tightly organized and succinct. It helps writers who know roughly what they want to cover but need to discover a way to bring diverse material together into a coherent whole. And it is well suited to writers who like to dictate. Dictation can take the place of a written first draft. The writer can listen to recorded thoughts, take notes, and organize the notes into an outline.

Many people dislike outlining; they find they can outline only *after* they've written a piece and seen what they want to say. The "Draft, Outline, Draft, Edit" approach acknowledges this reality and uses it to the writer's benefit. At the same time it avoids the looseness that usually results from writing successive drafts without outlining.

For pieces over three to five pages, however, this approach tends to be less successful. Writing a full rough draft of a longer piece takes much time and is often unnecessary if the writer has been immersed in the material for a lengthy period before sitting down to write.

THE SEVEN-STEP METHOD

This approach most closely approximates the "Think, Outline, Write" model but recognizes the inseparability of thinking and verbalizing. It encourages the writer to write while thinking and use notes to formulate an outline. It also allows writers to break long, complicated writing assignments into discrete steps that can be accomplished in relatively short periods. The seven steps are:

1. Information gathering, note-taking.

Immersion is the first step in any creative process. At this point, writers concentrate on reading, researching, and recording facts and statistics. The goal is to become thoroughly familiar with the topic and intellectually engaged in the material.

2. Incubating.

Here writers think, process information, jot down ideas, and discuss material with others. They also allow their minds to work on their material subconsciously.

3. *Planning.*

Next writers review jottings, notes, and lists and formulate an outline. The outline needn't be a formal affair with full sentences and roman numerals; it may be simply a list of issues, important pieces of information, and conclusions with arrows indicating a logical development.

4. *Drafting.*

Now the writer converts the outline into a narrative.

5. *Rest.*

All writers have trouble approaching their own prose from a reader's perspective. Immediately after finishing drafts, writers are too involved in their own ideas and words to hear how they will sound to readers. Always put work aside for at least several hours before trying to edit and revise systematically. The longer you let work rest before editing, the closer you will come to seeing it as a reader sees it.

6. *Revising, rewriting, editing.*

Writers should always schedule time for this step, usually more time than that allotted for writing the first draft. During this stage, writers concentrate on readability, persuasiveness, and correctness. They should examine their work systematically, looking for "red flags," which are recognizable symptoms of weakness in wording and organization. Chapters 3 and 4 of this book form a compendium of red flags to guide writers through systematic editing.

7. *Typing and proofing.*

Writers should take full responsibility for the final version of everything they write. "My secretary is a lousy typist" is a poor excuse for typos, sloppiness, spelling errors, or missing passages. Never let anything escape your office over your signature before proofing carefully. You will look like a bigger fool than your typist if your letters, memos, and reports contain errors. Also, if you value accuracy and neatness enough to correct typed drafts, your co-workers will soon adopt your values. But if *you* don't care, why should they?

THE EDITED SELF-INTERVIEW APPROACH

The traditional journalist's questions—who, what, where, when, and why—can be helpful to business writers, particularly when drafting short memos or reports to inform readers of routine matters. When writing to inform, these questions (the five W's) will help you include all the relevant information. They can also serve as a convenient method of organization. For example, if you pose these questions to yourself while writing to apprise your staff of a meeting, you'll be certain to specify who should attend, what the agenda will be, where and when the meeting will take place, and why attendance is important. Judicious use of the five W's can provide a quick, easy means of identifying and organizing important information.

After using the questions to compose a first draft, allow the draft to rest for a short period, then return to it for careful editing.

USING THE MODELS

Business writers should not rely exclusively on any one approach; in fact, the most successful writers will use aspects of several approaches while composing any given piece. A writer using the "Seven-Step Method" for a long report may, for example, use directed freewriting—quickly working through several drafts— to compose a difficult section of the report.

When first tackling a writing job, the writer should use the models as guides to thinking about the nature and requirements of the task. By recalling the models and choosing an appropriate one, the writer is forced to think explicitly about how much time to devote to a particular piece, how long the piece should be, what difficulties are likely to be encountered, and how polished the final piece should be. For example, a writer selecting the "Draft, Draft, Draft, . . . Edit" approach has determined that the final piece will be short, that there is enough time to work through several drafts, that the major challenge will be discovering what to say, and that the final product need not be a superior piece of prose.

Having selected one model as an overall approach, the writer should use this model to organize time. Each of the models breaks the job of writing into several parts. Thus, the models encourage people to view writing not as a single leap from blank page to final draft but as a series of steps, each of which is relatively small. Using models enables writers to formulate schedules in keeping with day-to-day demands of office work. Rarely can a businessperson devote eight uninterrupted hours to a task. Most businesspeople can, however, devote four intervals of two hours each to a task over the course of several days.

Finally, writers should use the models to suggest solutions to problems that occur while writing.

PROBLEMS THAT PLAGUE WRITERS

You need not be a professional writer to suffer from writer's block. Many people experience blocking as extreme difficulty in starting to write. Most of us also block occasionally in the midst of writing: we simply can't figure out what to say next.

All of the models combat blocking by making writing less formidable. Producing a 20-page report from a stack of blank sheets is a mind-boggling requirement. However, gathering information, reviewing files, and jotting down notes for an hour or two doesn't provoke anxiety. Nor does returning to notes later in the day to organize them into an outline.

Also, each model implicitly combats blocking by allowing time for material to rest between steps. These rest times allow writers to avail themselves of two wonderful prophylactics against blocking: the workings of the subconscious mind and the stimulation that comes from discussing work with others.

Accounts of creative breakthroughs in every field suggest that one's best ideas often surface when one is relaxed or consciously attending to something else. Some people solve problems best in the shower; others awaken from a good night's sleep and discover the answer to a deeply puzzling question. Once we've become immersed in our material—in information and ideas—our minds seem to work on problems by themselves.

Talking about work with others helps us become involved with what we're writing. It also forces us to start verbalizing ideas and explaining the results of our information-gathering to others. Thus, when we sit down to write after talking, words come more readily. Talking also gives ideas a critical prescreening and provides the writer with the benefit of outside perspectives. We may discover that an explanation we thought clear is far too convoluted for another to follow. We may also discover that a point we considered self-evident needs elaboration if it is to convince someone approaching it fresh.

Most of us naturally talk about our work when surrounded by co-workers. This natural tendency can become a deliberate strategy. All of the writing models presented in this chapter enable writers to talk about their writing projects between steps. Talking can also become a specific technique in the writer's repertoire of unblocking agents. Putting ideas into words for someone else often gets blocked writers back to their desks, eager to write.

Writers may have difficulty even after breaking jobs into manageable pieces and allowing time for rest and discussion. For such writers, directed freewriting ("Draft, Draft, Draft, . . . Edit") can be helpful. Freewriting encourages writers to view every draft as provisional; thus, it helps muffle the internal censoring voice that demands perfection and quashes every idea before it can get from the mind to the blank sheet. When the writer isn't aiming at perfection—a final draft—the ideas and words can flow more freely.

Freewriting also helps when writers reach impasses in the middle of their tasks. Here, too, it encourages a free flow of ideas and words, which enables the writer to discover what should come next.

Turning to the five W's can help writers who are blocked by uncertainty about whether they've said everything that needs saying or who don't know what to say next. Rereading what you have written, while keeping the five W's in mind, can help you identify what remains to be covered.

WRITING MODELS AND EDITING

No matter what approach you take to composition, you should make systematic editing a significant part of the process. Most writers edit and revise to some extent as they write. Getting clear about an idea and putting it into words often come to the same thing; to a large extent, finding expression for ideas is the same thing as discovering ideas. For this reason, writing and editing— generating ideas and looking critically at their expression in words—can never be completely separated. Yet each of the models discussed in this chapter includes editing as a final, distinct step in the production of documents.

When we write, we record ideas for ourselves, and our words often bring very clear images to our own minds. Our words may fail, however, to provoke the same clarity in the minds of readers. By editing systematically and with a fresh eye, we acknowledge the difference between expressing ideas adequately to ourselves and expressing them adequately to our readers.

An editor's goal is to view a piece of writing from

the reader's perspective. This goal can be difficult to reach for the editor who is also the author. For this reason, writers should let their manuscripts rest before returning to them as editors. The ability to recognize common symptoms of weakness in prose is even more important to the writer's success as an editor. For example, when you write a long sentence, you may have little difficulty understanding it: you composed it and know how you meant it to be read. But you can't trust your writer's ear to identify the sentence as potentially difficult for readers. During the editing phase, you should view all long sentences as potential reading problems. The long sentence is only one reading problem you should learn to identify. Many others are described in Chapters 3 and 4 of this book. The good writer-editor is aware of these problems and makes informed choices about them.

IDENTIFYING READERS AND THEIR NEEDS

Too many writers view composition as purely self-expression. Purely self-expressive writing may be art, but it isn't necessarily effective communication. When we write to communicate, we write to express ourselves *to readers.*

All people who write to communicate—whether they are novelists, journalists, or businesspeople—write to get results, though the desired results vary. Some people write to enlighten, inform, enchant, enrich, or entertain readers. Some people write to establish credibility, authority, or notoriety among readers. Others write to persuade readers to act in certain ways or accept certain beliefs. Business writers should constantly remind themselves that they're writing for readers to get *results.* The better you understand your readers and define the results you desire, the better your chances of achieving these results.

You'll often have two or more sets of readers, and they may have dissimilar interests, knowledge, values, and biases; readers with differing viewpoints are common in business. You may write a report for a client, but your boss may also read the report to evaluate your work. You may formulate reports destined for both clients and regulatory agencies. Or you may write a report to both the research staff and the production staff of your company.

When readers have different viewpoints or interests, you should be aware of the differences and make sure you address the concerns of your entire readership. You should also be careful not to alienate one group of readers inadvertently. For example, in a progress report you may want to share technical information with both co-workers and a client. Your client, however, may be unfamiliar with the jargon you routinely use with your colleagues. In this situation you should use jargon sparingly and define in nontechnical language each technical term you introduce.

Sometimes when your readers' interests, knowledge, and viewpoints differ significantly, composing two or more versions of a report, memo, or letter is your best solution. The growing availability of word processing equipment increases the feasibility of this approach. I've found that students who compose on computers or word processors are likely to prepare several versions of resumes and cover letters, gearing each version to the needs and culture of a particular organization.

Identifying readers, assessing their needs, and defining desired results are crucial to the business writer's success. The best way to accomplish these ends is to explore several questions about your readers and goals as you write.

1. *Who will read what you write?* List and picture *all* of your probable readers, including the secretary who screens the mail and the folks who will come across your memo in the files. Actually imagine readers perusing your work; you can avoid many potential problems with tone by picturing your readers' reactions to your words. As I mentioned previously, you may decide that your readers are so diverse that writing more than one version of your report or memo is appropriate.

2. *Who will act on what you write?* In some situations, you will have many readers, only one of whom will have authority to act on your recommendations. Although you should keep the needs of all readers in mind, make the needs of key readers your primary concern.

3. *What is your relationship to your readers?* Are you a peer, a superior, a subordinate? Is your reader a client, a supplier, a colleague? You speak differently to different people. The same should be true of your writing.

Different relationships call for different degrees of formality, openness, authority, and persuasiveness. Be sure to consider relationships from your readers' points of view. You may consider your readers peers, but they may consider themselves superiors. Perhaps one has held his position longer and another considers her function more important, even though you all occupy parallel rungs on the organizational ladder. Consider also what you'd like the relationship to be and how your letter or memo can help create the relationship you want.

4. *How do your readers perceive you, and what do they know about you?* Sometimes you'll be writing as an expert or authority, even though you may be writing to a superior. At other times you will be unknown to your readers and must introduce yourself and establish credibility.

If you're writing for your boss's signature, try to put yourself in his or her place: ask how your boss is perceived in the organization. When writing on behalf of your organization, ask how your readers view the organization.

5. *What do your readers know about your topic?* Belaboring the obvious and giving unnecessary background information can provoke annoyance. Not providing enough information, however, can be equally disastrous. Beware of inundating readers with information that serves no purpose. Many business writers obscure critical conclusions by burying them in heaps of pointless information. But remember that your readers will usually know less about your topic than you do; don't overestimate their knowledge.

6. *How much do your readers care about your topic?* Writers often forget that they may have more at stake than their readers. We've all become impatient reading memos, reports, letters, or brochures that assume we are infinitely fascinated by a topic that is, at most, of marginal interest to us. Gauge your readers'

involvement in your topic; it can help you make sound decisions about appropriate length and detail.

7. *What biases or attitudes will your reader bring to your topic?* Clarity, logical reasoning, and good evidence are sometimes not sufficient to secure a favorable reception for a message. Messages must often overcome barriers in the form of prejudices or preferences. Suppose you know that two associates hate meetings and you're drafting a letter urging them to attend the next gathering of the task force you're heading. You may do well to acknowledge their distaste immediately. You could, for example, begin your letter with, "I know you'd rather have four flat tires than put another meeting on your calendar, but. . . ."

Exploring your readers' biases can help you anticipate their objections to your position. If you foresee resistance, you will know where to build the strongest case through reasoning and evidence.

8. *What do you want your readers to do or know after reading?* When writing within organizations, we write to accomplish something: we write not to cover a topic but to achieve a goal. We want our readers to grant us an interview or to buy our services or to endorse our recommendations and act on them. Even when writing to inform, we're writing to inform decisions, not to increase our readers' general knowledge of a topic.

Before writing, try to picture in detail what you want your readers to do after they've finished your letter, memo, or report. Do you want them to call you and discuss what you've written or write back for more information? Do you want them to fill out the order form? Do you want them to grant you an interview when you call? Do you want them to form a task force or approve a loan? If, before you start writing, you can imagine what you want your reader to do, you'll be much better able to compose a piece that will achieve its purpose.

9. *If you had one sentence to summarize for your readers the main point of your letter, memo, or report, what would you say?* A summary sentence may read, "We should increase the price of product X because we're now losing money, our major competitors are charging more for similar products, and raising the price will increase our margins to retailers." A writer who formulates this kind of sentence will write about why the price of X should be increased, instead of about the pricing structure of product X.

10. *How will your writing be used?* Rarely does a piece of writing stand alone in the business world; it is usually part of a continuing relationship between reader and writer. Also, most writing in the business world has a mission beyond the initial reading. A memo to your boss may serve as the agenda for a meeting and then find its home in the files. Thinking about how your writing will actually be used will help you decide what to include and how to arrange material on the page.

View what you write within a larger context of ongoing communication. A report in which you recommend buying expensive new computers won't necessarily get you the new computers, but it may get you an opportunity to present your proposal to the senior staff at their next monthly meeting.

Many reports are too long and too detailed because their writers failed to see them as only one of many steps in securing action on their recommendations. Writers become unnecessarily anxious about letters, memos, and reports when they fail to see them in context. If you view your memo as a vehicle for initiating and directing discussion about a problem, you will make wiser decisions about what to say than if you view the memo as the final solution to a problem. You'll also be less likely to develop an ulcer.

Chapter 3

A Systematic Guide to Editing Sentences

WORD CHOICE

The difference between the almost right word and the right word is really a large matter —'tis the difference between the lightning bug and the lightning.
Mark Twain

MISTAKES IN USAGE

The richness of English allows writers to make subtle distinctions and to express ideas with precision. But opportunities for precision also represent occasions for error. English contains many troublesome words and phrases that cause problems because they are similar to other words and phrases in meaning, sound, or usage. Some examples of often confused words and phrases follow:

about—around
accept—except
adapt—adopt
admission—admittance
affect—effect
aggravate—annoy
among—between
amount—number
appraise—apprise
assure—ensure—insure
beside—besides
can—may
compare with—compare to
complement—compliment

council—counsel
disinterested—uninterested
eldest—oldest
farther—further
fortunate—fortuitous
fewer—less
flout—flaunt
hopefully—I hope
i.e.—e.g.
incredible—incredulous
infer—imply
its—it's
like—as
loathe—loath

loose—lose   stationary—stationery
precede—proceed   utilize—use
principal—principle   which—that

A reference on usage* should be part of every business writer's library, along with a dictionary and a thesaurus. Develop the habit of consulting these standard references when you're uncertain of a word's spelling or usage and when you suspect there may be a better word for what you want to say. Uncertainty is no crime. But making an error that you could easily have avoided suggests little respect for your reader, your message, and ultimately yourself.

The last two pairs of words in the list above, "utilize—use" and "which—that", are more often used improperly than properly in writing. "Utilize" suggests putting something to use that is normally discarded or using a familiar item in an unusual way. For example, garbage may be *utilized* to make bricks, or I may *utilize* my letter opener as a weapon to ward off an attacker. "Utilize" should be used only when the writer intends one of these two specific meanings. Otherwise, the better choice is "use."

"Which" and "that" are not interchangeable. "That" introduces defining phrases and clauses; "which" should be reserved for introducing phrases and clauses that give additional information about referents already unambiguously identified.

---

* Some good references on usage are: Theodore Bernstein, *The Careful Writer* (New York: Atheneum, 1982), available in paperback; H. W. Fowler, *A Dictionary of Modern English Usage* (New York: Oxford University Press, 1965), available in paperback.

"The copier *that* is in the closet is broken" suggests a different situation from "The copier, *which* is in the closet, is broken." The first sentence implies that there are several copiers; the phrase "that is in the closet" defines the one to which the writer wishes to refer. The second sentence suggests that there is only one copier; "which is in the closet" gives us additional information about this copier.

Clauses and phrases introduced by "which" should be set off with commas; commas should be omitted from phrases and clauses introduced by "that." If commas—pauses—sound wrong, chances are the proper word is "that."

The distinction between "which" and "that" is worth maintaining; by respecting it, writers can avoid troublesome ambiguity. When I was a technical editor for an engineering company, I often came across the following sentence in specifications (specifications are documents that specify to contractors and vendors the standards their work will have to meet): "The tests which will be performed by the XYZ Engineering Company are as follows." The sentence is ambiguous. Are all the tests going to be performed by XYZ? If so, the sentence should read, "The tests, which will be performed by the XYZ Engineering Company, are as follows." But commas are absent from the original, so the writer may intend to distinguish between tests that XYZ will perform and tests that the contractor or vendor will be required to perform. If the writer intends the second meaning, the sentence should read, "The tests that will be performed by the XYZ Engineering Company are as follows."

~ *Words are like leaves; and where they most abound*
Much fruit of sense beneath is rarely found.
Alexander Pope

UNNECESSARY WORDS

When executives are asked to name the major
weaknesses in the correspondence and reports they
read, one complaint consistently heads the list:
wordiness.

Surplus Words

Correct usage alone doesn't ensure readability.
Consider the (correct) sentence:

> Due to the fact that Tom, who was selected to head
> up our committee, arrived late, we were unable to
> reach a decision in the course of our meeting on
> whether or not to hold a product demonstration
> sometime next month.

Unnecessary verbiage clutters this sentence; a few re-
visions make it considerably shorter and more readable:

> Because Tom, who chairs our committee, arrived
> late, we were unable to decide at our meeting
> whether to hold a product demonstration next
> month.

Most writing contains sentences that can be improved
by crossing out unnecessary words or by substituting
single words for commonly used phrases. Wordiness is
not, however, a function of the length of a sentence. "He
leafed through *the pages of* the annual report" is wordy,

though it contains only nine words: "the pages of" is unnecessary. The test of wordiness isn't whether a sentence contains many words but whether every word in the sentence serves a purpose.

Streamlining sentences takes practice and imagination. The writer can begin by looking for common phrases and constructions that signal wordiness:

> "Due to the fact that" and "in view of" can be reduced to "because."
>
> "Whether or not" is often unnecessary— "whether" is usually sufficient.
>
> "In the course of" can be shortened to "during."
>
> "Head up" (as in "head up a committee") should stop at "head." The same principle applies to many "_____-up" compounds, like "start up" and "finish up."
>
> "The manner in which" can be changed to "the way."
>
> "In order to" can usually be left at "to. . . ."

Wordy	Better
advance plan	plan
action plan	plan
take action	act
have a discussion	discuss
hold a meeting	meet
study in depth	study
at the present time	now
until such time as	until
in the majority of instances	most
on a local basis	locally

Wordy	Better
in the area of	approximately or about
at the management level	by management
with regard to	about or concerning
in connection with	of, in, or on
in view of	because
in the event of	if
for the purpose of	for
on the basis of	by or from
despite the fact that	although
in the majority of instances	usually
hold in abeyance	wait or postpone
accompanied by	with
affix your signature	sign
afford an opportunity	allow or permit
as of this day	today
at an early date	soon
in compliance with your request	as requested
subsequent to	after
time differential	delay
due to the fact that	because

Unnecessary Subordination

Sometimes wordiness results from the way a writer structures a sentence. Subordinate clauses (groups of words beginning with relative pronouns—who, which, that—or subordinating conjunctions—when, where, although, because, since, while, etc.) can often be shortened to prepositional phrases or appositives. Don't panic at all this talk of clauses, phrases, appositives, and subordination: some things are harder to talk about than to do. Here are some examples of clauses converted to phrases:

> The statistics *that were* compiled by the Research Department are reliable.
>
> The statistics compiled by the Research Department are reliable.
>
> My friend, *who is* a professor of Marketing, is writing a book.
>
> My friend, a professor of Marketing, is writing a book.
>
> *While we were having* our meeting on the new ad campaign, Joe suggested *that we* consider comic books as a medium for advertising.
>
> During our meeting on the new ad campaign, Joe suggested considering comic books as a medium for our advertising.

You can't convert every subordinate clause into a phrase. But as you edit, look for words that introduce subordinate clauses and play with the sentences in which they occur. You'll often find that these sentences can be reduced to shorter, more direct statements.

Unnecessary Modification

After you've crossed out all the obviously surplus words, found all the phrases that can be shortened to single words, and eliminated structural wordiness lurking in subordinate clauses, you may still be left with wordy sentences. Modifiers—adjectives, adverbs, and intensifiers—frequently make sentences longer but not more meaningful.

Sometimes adjectives and adverbs can be eliminated by selecting precise nouns and verbs. For example, "The TV played loudly" can be rewritten "The TV blared." Writers not familiar with the precise meanings and usages of words often add modifiers whose meanings are contained in the nouns and verbs of a sentence. "He clenched his fist tightly" is redundant: "to clench" means "to hold tightly."

In the sentence "By fortuitous accident, I bumped into Jack," "fortuitous" is unnecessary because it means "accidental."

Redundant	Better
new innovations	innovations
consensus of opinion	consensus
interim period	interim
and/or	(use one or the other)
cooperate together	cooperate
small in size	small
basic essentials	essentials
descended down	descended
worthy of merit	worthy
visible to the eye	visible
circle around	circle

Intensifiers. Short words or phrases that answer in a general way the question "How much?" or "To what extent?" are intensifiers. They include "very," "rather," "quite," "too," and "a bit." Consider such words candidates for red-pencilling. A paper sprinkled with intensifiers indicates an insecure writer. Sentences like

"Competition was rather intense" appear when writers feel uncertain of their assertions and conclusions. A confident writer will say "Competition was intense" and go on to present evidence supporting the assertion. If the facts don't support a strong adjective like "intense," the writer should change the sentence to "Competition was moderate." Intensifiers can, of course, serve legitimate purposes. "Very" adds emphasis when used sparingly; "rather," "quite," and "a bit" may be necessary to limit statements. If you use intensifiers thoughtfully, those you use will serve their intended purposes—adding emphasis to statements or limiting them.

Irrelevant information in modifiers. Writers sometimes pack sentences with information by using modifiers (phrases as well as single-word adjectives and adverbs). Often the information is useful, but not in the sentence in which it appears. Consider this sentence:

Rockwell entered the *intensely competitive, disorganized* market for pocket calculators in 1974.

The above sentence provides information that the following sentence does not:

Rockwell entered the market for pocket calculators in 1974.

But what is the main point of the first sentence: that Rockwell entered the market in 1974 or that the market was competitive and disorganized?

Modifiers that add information irrelevant to the central point of a sentence dilute the point and distract the reader. Either put this information into separate sentences or leave it out. Rather than writing "Rockwell entered the intensely competitive, disorganized market for pocket calculators in 1974," write:

> Rockwell entered the market for pocket calculators in 1974. At that time, the market was intensely competitive and disorganized.

Coupled Synonyms

Common in legal writing, coupled synonyms sometimes find their way into business writing:

> acknowledge and confess
> final and conclusive
> fit and proper
> peace and quiet
> have and hold
> just and reasonable
> last will and testament

Only one word from each pair is necessary, since both words have about the same meaning.

Sometimes synonyms coupled by "or" sneak into first drafts because writers aren't certain of exactly what they want to say:

> The *idea or purpose* of this measure is to increase productivity.

As you edit, search for coupled synonyms. When you decide what you mean to say, you'll find that a single word will do quite well:

> The purpose of this measure is to increase productivity.

∿ *Abstract nouns are the barbituates of communication: soporific in small doses and lethal in large ones.*
Anthony Jay, The New Oratory.

POMPOUS LANGUAGE

Businesspeople often think they must adopt a special vocabulary whenever they write. This vocabulary differs from their normal speech and usually results in prose that sounds stiff, impersonal, and condescending; in a word, pompous.

Inflated and Pretentious Wording

Inflation is a problem in our society—in our language as well as in our economy. We are no longer *aware* of things; we are *cognizant* of them. We don't do things *now;* we do them *currently, at this point in time,* or *presently.* We don't *use* things; we must *utilize* them. We mustn't have a *first* reaction: instead we must have an *initial* reaction. Our woes can't be *many:* they must be *numerous.* No longer may we *say yes;* instead we must *answer in the affirmative.* Clearly, word inflation is a problem *of considerable magnitude,* not simply a *large* problem. But improvement is *within the realm of possibility,* which is far better than being merely *possible.*

Word inflation and pretentious language have many sources. Chief among them is dishonesty—a desire to obscure meaning or misrepresent one's position, certainty, knowledge, or attitude. Listen to Hodding Carter "answer" a reporter's question:

> You are trying to get me to make policy in advance of a situation arising which does not now pertain.
> *New York Times,* December 5, 1979

39

Inflated language also results from the mistaken notion that obscure language connotes knowledge, wisdom, authority. Here is Pope John Paul II, the man who charmed millions of common folk on his tour of the world, writing in a scholarly journal:

> While somatic dynamism and indirectly the psycho-emotive dynamism have their source in the body matter, this source is neither sufficient nor adequate for the action in its essential feature of transcendence.
>
> As quoted in *Newsweek*

In *Writing for Results,* David Ewing provides two wonderful examples of pretentious wording: "motorized attendance modules" (for school buses) and "interior intrusion detection systems" (the Pentagon's lingo for burglar alarms).

Overuse of abstract words.

Word inflation, pretentious language, and abstractions (concept words) go hand-in-hand. The Pope's passage is full of abstract words—"dynamism," "psycho-emotive," "body-matter," "transcendence." But the Pope is not alone. A student begins a paper for a class in business policy with:

> There is no more emotive subject occupying the collective minds of the emerging communal society than that of pollution.

"Emotive subject," "collective mind," "communal society"—what do these terms mean? They probably meant something to the author of the passage, but they are too abstract to suggest much to the reader who isn't also a mind reader. Abstract words shouldn't be used to make a simple statement sound profound. The student writing of emotive subjects, collective minds, and communal society probably meant to say something like:

> Many people are concerned about pollution, but they disagree on what should be done about it.

Careless use of abstract words may obscure your message and make you look like an ass. But abstract words present an even greater risk—that of dead-ending your own thinking. Concept words can be thought traps. Many essays, reports, and memos never progress beyond abstraction; they don't develop themes so much as tediously restate them in different abstract terms.

Buzzwords

When an abstract or technical term becomes trendy, it becomes a buzzword. Buzzwords sound pretentious; moreover, they don't say anything. Try to describe the program the author of the following sentence has in mind:

> We need to develop a program *compatible* with the structure of our organization and *responsive* to its needs.

"Compatible" and "responsive" are perfectly good words, but do they say anything in the above sentence? Think for a moment. How many organizations strive to design programs *incompatible* with their structures and *unresponsive* to their needs? Not many successful ones.

Some writers cynically use buzzwords to inflate the obvious or to conceal gaps in thought or knowledge. Other writers use buzzwords unwittingly, not realizing that the words they've chosen fail to communicate their ideas. Many writers resort to buzzwords when trying to compress a complex jumble of ideas into a single word or phrase. The writer who wants a compatible, responsive program may have had some specific constraints in mind when composing. But the writer's specific concerns don't find expression in the sentence.

Below is a list of buzzwords commonly used in business and government. Bear in mind that a word becomes a buzzword by virtue of context: all of the listed words have legitimate uses, though most of the words should be avoided because they are overused.

optimize	centralize	implement
maximize	decentralize	projection
minimize	responsive	contingency
effectualize	compatible	impact
prioritize	doable	interface
finalize	achievable	output
logistical	systematize	viable
incremental	functional	feedback
options	organizational	and/or
concept	management	per
time-phase	input	parameters
time-frame		

Examine your work for buzzwords. Use the list above as a guide, but don't stop with these words. Look for trendy words, vague words. Ask whether these words communicate your thoughts unambiguously. Ask whether other words or more thorough explanation would get your point across more accurately.

∿ *American jargon is such fun to contemplate, so*
full of pompous self-satisfaction on the one hand
and cynical, knowing, ritual mystification on the
other that description hardly knows where to
begin. . . .
> *. . . a student* [can't] *cut off the daily flow*
of jargon he drowns in. But he can be taught to
recognize it, see through it, even laugh at it.
R. Lanham *Style: An Anti-Textbook*

JARGON

We all laugh at other groups' jargon, but most of us
feel that the jargon in our own field is absolutely necessary for accuracy and economy of expression. We feel
annoyed and perhaps amused if a doctor says, "You are
suffering from a form of contact dermatitis resulting
from exposure to certain plants of the genus *Toxico-
dendron*." Yet we'll turn around, cursing the poison ivy
between our fingers, and write of milking a company's
cash cow to nourish the *problem child.*

Jargon is the language of specialists and is appropriate when writing or speaking to other specialists in the
same field. People conversant in a jargon usually aren't
offended by it. But a writer should *never* assume a
reader's familiarity with jargon. Don't make the mistake
of assuming that "anyone who knows anything about
business will know what I mean when I write of cash
cows." Don't bet on it. Jargon tends to be more local
than you think, and many successful executives have
never heard of cash cows and would prefer not to.

Once you're sure your audience will understand
your jargon, make sure *you* understand it. Nothing
makes a writer look more foolish than improper use of

jargon. Before you get carried away by jargon, make sure you know where you're going. If you aren't sure of the meaning or usage of a technical term, don't use it.

A final caution about jargon: like concept words, jargon can get in the way of clear thinking. Having identified a product as a "cash cow," many people will write about cash cows generally, forgetting the specific product and situation they're writing about. Avoid this mistake. If you can't say it in plain English, you don't fully understand what you're talking about.

Business writing contains much jargon. Identify the jargon you've used, then ask yourself whether it is necessary. Could your point have been made more clearly and concisely without the jargon? Like the doctor, might you have said, "You've got poison ivy"?

SENTENCE STRUCTURE

∼ *The difference between an active-verb style and
a passive-verb style —in pace, clarity, and vigor —
is the difference between life and death for a
writer.*

*Verbs are the most important of all your tools.
They push the sentence forward and give it mo-
mentum. Active verbs push hard; passive verbs tug
fitfully.*

William Zinsser, *On Writing Well*

THE PASSIVE SENTENCE

In a passive sentence or clause, the subject does nothing; instead, something is done to the subject. The preceding sentence contains both active and passive constructions: "the subject does nothing" is active; "something is done to the subject" is passive. Overuse of passive sentence structure mars much business writing. Passive has its place, but its place is smaller than most writers think. You should use passive when the object of an action is more important than the subject. If someone asks, "When was the letter sent?" you'll probably reply, "The letter was sent yesterday" (passive). The structure of your reply reflects the importance of the *letter:* the questioner doesn't want to know *who* sent the letter, so the logical subject of the sentence—the implied sender—is not important. If, however, you're asked, "Who sent the letter," you'll probably reply, "I sent the letter" (active), rather than, "The letter was sent by me" (passive). In this example, the sender of the letter deserves emphasis.

Passive voice doesn't obscure meaning when the subject of an action is unimportant, unknown, or clearly implied. But many passive sentences are ambiguous. In business reports and memos, one often finds sentences like: "The market is projected to grow at a rate of 15% a year." The writer doesn't tell the reader where the projection comes from. Did the writer arrive at the projection after looking at Nielsen reports, or does the projection come from a trade journal? Perhaps consultants provided the projection. The reader can only guess.

When passive doesn't entail ambiguity, it often requires unnecessary words:

The calculator industry in 1974 was characterized

by high-quality products and decreasing prices. (Passive: 14 words)

High-quality products and decreasing prices characterized the calculator industry in 1974. (Active: 12 words)

In this example, converting passive to active both shortens the sentence and places emphasis where it belongs— on the characteristics of the market.

If you eliminate passive whenever possible, your writing will become more direct, more interesting, more colorful—in short, more compelling.

∼ *Simple English is no one's mother tongue. It has to be worked for.*
Jacques Barzun

EXPLETIVES

There are many writers who begin sentences as I've begun this one—with an expletive. An expletive sentence (or clause) is one in which "there are" or "it is" appears in place of a subject.

Expletives usually make sentences longer than they need be. Moreover, expletives shift the emphasis of a sentence from the main point to a meaningless phrase— "it is" or "there are":

There are many reasons for us to expect unit sales to decrease by 20% a year.

This should be revised to:

> We expect unit sales to decrease by 20% a year for many reasons.

The second version is shorter than the first and gets to the writer's main point more quickly.

~ *See if you can gain variety by reversing the order of a sentence, by substituting a word that has freshness or oddity, by altering the length of your sentences so that they don't all sound as if they came out of the same computer. An occasional short sentence can carry a tremendous punch. It stays in the reader's ear.*
William Zinsser, *On Writing Well*

LENGTH

The next time you find yourself dozing over a book, report, memo, or article, check the length of its sentences. Often, you'll find that the sentences are all about the same length. Variation keeps readers awake. By varying the length of your sentences, you can maintain your readers' attention. Variety is not, however, the sole determinant of appropriate sentence length.

Long sentences require more of readers than short sentences: readers must concentrate harder to read and comprehend long sentences. In familiar, nontechnical material, long sentences cause readers the fewest headaches. In complex, abstract, or technical writing, however, a sentence may become insufferable far before it reaches a period.

If you tend to write in long sentences, read your writing out loud; your ear picks up difficulties your eye misses. When you stumble in the middle of a sentence, try breaking it into two or three shorter sentences.

You can help your reader through long sentences by structuring and punctuating them carefully: keep modifiers close to what they modify; avoid passive and expletive structures; guide your reader with accurate punctuation.

As an inspiration to shorter, more readable sentences, I leave you with:

> The projected volume decline of 9% in Phase Two is viewed as an ambitious goal in light of the following factors: a) an increasing competitive environment with Energade facing two major competitors (namely Tummylicious, which has superior dissolving and taste characteristics vis-a-vis Energade, and Tastytime, which has more than doubled its share of market in 1976); b) the expected heavy media support for Tummylicious and other competitive brands resulting in Energade no longer dominating category spending (Energade share of voice declining from 65% in 1975 to 43% in 1976 declining to an estimated 30% in 1977); and c) uncertainty as to the precise volume impact of the price increase to 49¢ for Energade, which is heavily reliant on teenage/young-adult purchase, and the impact of the midyear increase to 59¢ on Sugarless Energade, approximately one year after its introduction nationally in 1976.

GRAMMAR AND PUNCTUATION

> ∿ *All alumni of old Harvard Law*
> *Are true gems, whether polished or raw;*
> *So why all this clamor*
> *About their poor grammar*
> *When their briefs is the finest I've saw?*
> E. Schein, as quoted in *Writing for Results*

Perhaps grads of old Harvard Law can afford to overlook grammar, but most of us cannot. Grammatical errors make writers look careless; they tell a reader the writer doesn't care enough to express ideas correctly. Errors also reduce clarity. Below, I've listed and briefly described the rules of grammar and punctuation I've seen most often violated in business writing.

1. *Pronouns should have clear antecedents.* When in doubt, repeat the antecedent to avoid confusion like the following:

> Linda and Jim outlined three marketing plans for the clients, and they later discussed them with top management.

This could mean:

> Linda and Jim outlined three marketing plans for the clients, and the clients later discussed the plans with top management.

Or it could mean:

> Linda and Jim outlined three marketing plans for

the clients and later discussed the plans with top management.

Or it could mean:

Linda and Jim outlined three marketing plans for the clients, who later discussed Linda and Jim with top management.

Or it could mean:

Linda and Jim outlined three marketing plans for the clients and then discussed the clients with top management.

When in doubt, repeat the antecedent.

2. *Subjects and predicates should agree in number.* The verb in a sentence or clause should agree with the subject, not with the nearest noun:

The *frustration* of ad agency work—the long hours, frequent interruptions, relatively low wages, and many deadlines—*is* small compared to the rewards.

Use singular verbs with "each," "either," "everyone," "everybody," "neither," "nobody," and "someone."

3. *A participial phrase, appositive, adjective, or adjectival phrase that begins a sentence should refer to the subject of the sentence.*

Incorrect: Tired and frustrated, a vacation appealed to Linda.
Correct: A vacation appealed to Linda, who felt tired and frustrated.

Incorrect: Although out of gas, Martha tried to drive the car.

Correct: Martha tried to drive the car although it was out of gas.

4. *An introductory phrase, clause, or transitional word should be separated from the rest of the sentence by a comma.*

Incorrect: Because Ajax Company must reduce its advertising budget ad campaigns will be curtailed.

Correct: Because Ajax Company must reduce its advertising budget, ad campaigns will be curtailed.

Incorrect: An enthusiastic worker Tom never misses a day.

Correct: An enthusiastic worker, Tom never misses a day.

Incorrect: Moreover all of our employees are covered by our pension plan.

Correct: Moreover, all of our employees are covered by our pension plan.

Incorrect: During next month's meeting in New York we will reveal our new line of products.

Correct: During next month's meeting in New York, we will reveal our new line of products.

The comma is optional, however, in sentences introduced by a single, short prepositional phrase:

Correct: At the annual dinner my boss announced bonuses for the entire staff.

5. *Commas should separate items in a series.* Whether the items are nouns, verbs, modifiers, or phrases, they should be set off from one another with commas.

Example: Three brands dominate the market for soft bubble gum: Bubble Yum, Hubba Bubba, and Bubblelicious.

Example: Wise executives review their daily activities in the shower, on the way to work, and before going to bed.

Example: The company will lower prices, increase margins, and advertise heavily.

6. *Independent clauses joined by a coordinating conjunction should be punctuated with a comma before the conjunction.* The words "and," "but," "or," "nor," and "for" are coordinating conjunctions.

Example: We're directing our advertising toward mothers, for they are the primary purchasers of Pampers.

7. *Independent clauses not joined by a coordinating conjunction should be separated by a semicolon.*

Example: The demand for natural foods is growing; our company should take advantage of this growth.

Example: We plan to attend the meeting; however, we doubt we'll learn much.

8.   Parenthetic expressions should be set off with commas. A parenthetic expression is an "unnecessary" interruption in a sentence. Think of parenthetic expressions as asides that you might enclose in parentheses.

> Example: We're promoting Tom Robbins, who joined our company last May, to Vice-President of Sales.

The expression "who joined our company last May" is parenthetical: it is not needed to identify what it modifies—Tom Robbins.

A group of words needed to identify or define what it modifies is not parenthetic and should *not* be set off with commas.

> Example: Those who joined our company last May will begin receiving fringe benefits in January.

A Guide to Editing for Organization and Structure: The Paragraph

*⁓ The order of ideas in a . . . paragraph should
be such that the reader need not rearrange them
in his mind.*

Robert Graves and Alan Hodge, *The Reader Over Your Shoulder*

CHARACTERISTICS OF GOOD
PARAGRAPHS

Paragraphs are conceptual packages that group and organize ideas for readers. A well-formed paragraph is purposeful, complete, unified, orderly, and coherent. Few people naturally think in well-formed paragraphs, so to create a good paragraph, most writers must consciously strive to achieve these characteristics.

By examining paragraphs while editing, you can identify both potential difficulties for readers and gaps in your own reasoning.

PURPOSE

"Purpose" describes the function of a paragraph within a presentation. A paragraph may be well structured—internally coherent—yet fail to serve a clearly communicated purpose.

The example paragraph below comes from a student's paper. Note that it is focused—it has a topic and sticks to that topic—and that it moves logically from one point to the next. It is not, however, purposeful. The writer either had no purpose in mind when writing the paragraph or failed to communicate the purpose.

By 1974 total U.S. calculator sales had grown to about 12 million units annually. Unit sales had grown at a compound rate of about 188% per year from 1971 to 1974, while dollar sales grew 89% per year. At the same time, the average unit price dropped from $200 to $57. Although it was projected that unit growth would slow to approximately 20–25% annually for the next several years, it was also estimated that prices would continue to drop at about the same rate, resulting in an annual decline in dollar sales of 5–7% in 1975 and 1976.

The so-called "So what?" test can help you determine whether a paragraph has a purpose. Ask yourself what each paragraph does in terms of your presentation as a whole: what does it establish, assert, conclude, or explain? Make sure that you haven't simply thrown your readers a list of facts.

COMPLETENESS

Every paragraph should include the supporting detail, evidence, and explanation necessary to achieve its purpose and to communicate its purpose clearly.

The characteristics of your audience will largely determine what you must include in a paragraph to make it complete. When writing to a superior, you may have to establish your credibility with skillful use of evidence and perceptive analysis. When presenting ideas to a colleague or subordinates, you may be less concerned with credibility but more concerned with clarity. To achieve your goal with a hostile audience, you must provide a good bit of evidence and explanation; a friendly audience, however, will demand less of you. Well-informed audiences won't need as much background information to understand your points as will uninformed audiences. But an informed audience may be more critical, quicker to spot gaps in your logic or to recall information you've disregarded.

There's an old saying among journalists, "Never underestimate your readers' intelligence and never overestimate their knowledge." When you are writing to persuade rather than to inform, you might modify the journalist's adage to read, "Never underestimate your readers' intelligence but never overestimate their sympathy with your position."

UNITY

A unified paragraph introduces a topic and sticks to it. Unity and purpose are closely related. Paragraphs that contain digressions and those that slowly but surely drift away from the main point (i.e., un-unified paragraphs) occur when writers haven't identified the purpose of their paragraphs.

Under the heading "The Company's Objectives," a writer included this paragraph:

> The executives wish to have a 12% market share by the fall of 1975, and hope to gain this by establishing the ABC line in 34 introductory target markets for a total of 736 outlets. The machine cosmetics were designed to help consumers develop a strong brand awareness. They also hope to maintain a reputation for high quality and reliability by having less than 3% customer returns. Due to frequent price changes, which cause problems to retailers, ABC management also has liberal stock adjustment and price-change policies. A program to train retail salespeople is considered to be essential, and there is a cooperative advertising campaign that allows for up to 3% of a retailer's net purchases. ABC is

offering better retail and wholesale prices than XYZ and is offering retailer margins of 28% to 40%. Management is considering anticipating XYZ's move into the mass-merchandiser market, and this would mean increasing the advertising budget to $5 million and an increase in sales and distribution costs to $4 million.

The paragraph begins well, stating ABC's share-of-market goal. By the second sentence, however, the writer has wandered into the topic of how machine cosmetics will help attain this goal by creating brand awareness. The third sentence seems to introduce another objective—maintaining a reputation for quality. But the fourth sentence discusses ABC's current stock and price-change policies. Since the writer has begun to talk about relationships with retailers in the fourth sentence, the fifth sentence takes up the matter of training salespeople and conducting cooperative ad campaigns. The next sentence takes the retailer-manufacturer theme a step further, discussing ABC's margins as compared to XYZ's. The final sentence follows the XYZ thread and introduces the issue of beating XYZ to the mass merchandisers.

The writer has consistently drifted from the main concern—identifying and articulating ABC's goals. The drift isn't illogical—each sentence picks up on an idea in a previous sentence—but the paragraph ends on a theme quite different from the one on which it began.

ORDER

A well-structured paragraph moves consistently in a discernible direction, though this direction (the principle of order) need not be stated explicitly.

Paragraphs may be ordered in several ways. Time may be the ordering principle in a paragraph reviewing past actions. A time-ordered paragraph may move from past to present or may work from the present back to the past. Space is another common ordering principle, especially in passages describing physical arrangements. A writer describing the layout of a boiler room might begin by describing what a viewer would see upon entering the room and then describe what the viewer would see by looking to the left or right. Or the writer might begin with a bird's-eye view of the room's shape and then discuss the placement of individual pieces of machinery within the room. The important point is consistency—choosing a principle of order and sticking to it.

Most of the paragraphs you write will require a conceptual principle of order rather than a temporal or spatial one. You may move from general to particular, particular to general, question to answer, effect to cause, or assertion to support. Sometimes your paragraphs may develop contrasts; they may present one point of view, develop it, shift to a contrasting point of view, and conclude by reconciling the points of view or rejecting one of them. But whatever principle of order you choose for a paragraph, stick to it.

COHERENCE

Paragraphs lacking unity and order also lack coherence. A paragraph may be unified and ordered, however, and still be incoherent. Coherence is partly a function of the conceptual integrity of the paragraph, but it is also a function of the writer's skill in communicating the unity and order of a paragraph to the reader.

Several devices can help writers highlight the coherence of paragraphs for readers.

Topic Sentences

A topic sentence tells a reader what a paragraph is about. But a good topic sentence does more than introduce a topic by mentioning it. Think of a topic sentence as the most important statement you can make about the material in a paragraph. A topic sentence can appear almost anywhere in a paragraph, but it usually occurs near the beginning or the end. When you're moving from general to particular, your topic sentence will probably appear at the beginning of the paragraph; when you're moving from particular to general, your topic sentence will probably be the concluding sentence in your paragraph. Sometimes a topic sentence appears at the start of a paragraph and is repeated at the end of the paragraph (i.e., the main point of the paragraph is stated at the outset and restated, in different terms, at the end). Regardless of where the topic sentence occurs, every paragraph should have one.

Connectives

A topic sentence emphasizes a paragraph's unifying principle or theme. But readers frequently need additional signals to follow the writer's thought from sentence to sentence within a paragraph. Connectives provide these signals.

Connectives are words and phrases like:

therefore
thus
however

in addition
also
furthermore
on the other hand
and
but
first
second

They tell readers whether to expect a conclusion, a related point, a contrasting idea, or the next in a series of points. Connectives can't make a paragraph ordered or unified; the word "therefore" can't create a logical entailment that doesn't exist, and "furthermore" doesn't magically convert a digression into a logical continuation. But connectives can highlight for readers the logical progression of your thought, providing your thought follows some logical progression to begin with.

Connections without Connectives

Connectedness, coherence, and logical progression can be communicated without using explicit connectives. Relationships between ideas can be emphasized by parallel or similar sentence structures. Take, for example:

> We want to increase our sales. We also want to control our growth. Expanding our distribution system is another important goal. We want to be sure, however, to maintain good relations with our current distributors.

Instead, you might write:

> We want to increase our sales, but we also want to

control our growth. We want to expand our distribution network, but we also want to maintain good
relations with our current distributors.

In the second version, similar sentence structures emphasize logical relationships: the goal of increasing sales
is paired with the constraint of controlling growth, and
the goal of expanding distribution is paired with the
constraint of maintaining good relationships.

Repeating key words or explicitly referring to
points previously made in a paragraph can also convey
and reinforce logical connections. For example:

Consultants expect sales of cassettes to reach 2
million units a year by 1980. The market for cassettes can be divided into three segments. . . .

Instead, you could write:

Consultants expect the *market* for cassettes to
reach 2 million units a year by 1980. *This market*
can be divided into three segments. . . .

The second version is more coherent than the first,
though both versions communicate the same information in the same order. Repetition of the key word
"market" in the second reinforces the logic of moving
from the size of the total market into a discussion of how
the market is segmented.

Repetition should be used sparingly. Repeating key
words adds emphasis and coherence but gets monoto-
nous quickly. In fact, you should look for inadvertent
repetition as you edit because it often signals wordiness
or an opportunity for greater variety.

SPECIAL PARAGRAPHS

A paragraph that begins a letter, memo, or report generally differs from paragraphs that occur in the body. The opening paragraph, which may introduce the writer, convey greetings, or summarize major points, deserves special attention.

SELF-INTRODUCTION OR GREETING

Letters frequently begin with paragraphs of introduction or greeting. These paragraphs may introduce an unfamiliar writer (as in a cover letter) or make a conversational reference to a previous meeting or social occasion or to personal matters. However, writers should introduce their main points either at the end of these paragraphs or at the beginning of the second paragraph.

SUMMARIZING AND EXECUTIVE SUMMARIES

The first paragraph of a report often summarizes conclusions presented in the main body. A good first paragraph does so by stating the thesis of the piece and the major supporting points in an order that reflects the organization of the report or memo as a whole.

The sample paragraph below illustrates how a good first paragraph can introduce a topic, state a thesis and the major findings that support it, and give the reader a preview of a report's organization:

> Many of our managers seem to resist the new desktop computers, but their resistance stems from the problems they're experiencing rather than from

"terminal terror." Several departments have received defective equipment, and managers have had to spend valuable time debugging systems because of poor quality control in manufacture. In addition, many of our managers report that the instructions accompanying both hardware and software are distinctly user unfriendly. Finally, many managers complain about the dizzying array of software, firmware, and peripherals and the lack of compatibility among them. Managers feel they haven't time to do the research and experimenting necessary to select the best systems for their departments' needs.

The first sentence of the paragraph identifies the topic of the report—managers' reactions to the desktop computers being introduced in their company. It also states the report's thesis—managers are reluctant to embrace the new technology because they're having problems with it rather than because they suffer from terminal terror. Each of the next three sentences details a problem managers have experienced; the order in which the writer presents the problems in this paragraph reflects the order in which they are presented in the body of the report.

A good first paragraph is almost impossible to formulate until you have composed the rest of your memo or report. You can save yourself unnecessary misery by bearing this in mind as you write drafts; don't agonize over the first paragraph until you're satisfied with the rest of the piece.

Executive summaries perform much the same functions as a first paragraph but are usually longer. An executive summary may consist of several paragraphs or even several pages in a long report. Like the first paragraph, the executive summary is easiest to write when you've finished the rest of a report and know, therefore, what you have to summarize.

Besides differing in length, executive summaries may also differ in amount of detail. They are generally meant to stand alone and are often directed to readers whom the writer assumes will not read further. As a result, they often provide somewhat more detail than an opening paragraph. A good way to determine what belongs in an executive summary is to ask yourself what you want your readers to see, assuming they will go no further.

FROM PARAGRAPHS TO PRESENTATIONS

Most memos, letters, and reports should begin with the most important conclusion, recommendation, or point of information for the reader. Because conclusions come last in our thinking, we often want to put them at the end of what we write. Readers, however, generally want to get to the main points first. Then they can decide whether to read on immediately for details, route the document to someone else, or return to it later for careful reading. They can also determine whether immediate action or filing for reference is appropriate. Putting the most important points up front also facilitates future use of the documents you compose. When going through the files, co-workers can skim your first paragraph and determine whether your document is relevant to the question at hand. Finally, by beginning with your conclusions, you can often predispose readers to reach the same ones while reading through the body of your memo or report.

A presentation is *logically organized* when one portion follows logically from the last portion and leads logically to the next. A presentation is *well organized* when it is organized logically with the reader's interests and needs in mind.

To check the logic of your organization, ask whether each paragraph leads to the topic discussed in the next paragraph. If you often find no connection, you could probably find a better organization for your ideas and information. Also check to see whether you discuss the same topic in more than one place. If you do, you may find opportunities to combine discussions and rearrange them so that you needn't return to topics already considered.

～ . . . *paragraphs should be linked together logically and intelligibly.*

Graves and Hodge, *The Reader Over Your Shoulder*

TRANSITIONS

Transitions are verbal expressions of logical and thematic connections. A transitional sentence, for example, highlights the logical or thematic relationship between topics discussed in adjacent paragraphs. Transitions help readers follow thoughts; they help writers reinforce important points.

Suppose you have written a paragraph on the Gizmo market—its current size, projections for growth, and so on—and you want to discuss segmentation of the Gizmo market in your next paragraph. The first sentence in your second paragraph—the transition—might be, "Although the total market for Gizmos is shrinking, some segments of the market are expanding." The transitional sentence emphasizes the logical progression of your thought. It points to the logic of considering first the market as a whole and then how the market is segmented.

Transitions come in forms other than sentences. An entire paragraph may serve as a transition between major sections of a report. Transitions may also be less than a sentence. Single-word connectives, parallel sentence structure, or repetition of key words and themes can also serve as transitions between paragraphs.

Try to make your transitions as economical as possible. Look for key words to repeat or single-word connectives before resorting to a full sentence. Also, try to make your transitions do as much work as possible. Look for opportunities to make topic sentences serve as transitions. In the Gizmo example, the transition not only highlights a logical connection but also introduces the topic of the next paragraph and communicates an important point—that some segments of the market are expanding.

Transitions cannot create a logical connection where none exists. As a friend of mine once said, "It's hard to write a good transition between cows and Ping-Pong balls." If there's no logical or thematic connection to highlight, don't force a transition. If you find yourself continually forcing transitions, recheck the organization of your paper. When transitions are difficult to formulate, poor organization is often the culprit.

FORMAT

A good format can help a writer convey logical relationships, express ideas economically, emphasize important points, and make a presentation attractive to read. When you have substantial control of format (writers in many organizations are tightly bound to detailed format rules), you should consider using the following devices:

> white space
> headings
> lists
> indenting, underlining, and capitalizing

White Space

A page that is black with type looks formidable. Ample margins and space between sections make memos, letters, and reports more inviting to readers and, thus, more likely to be read.

Headings

Headings allow readers to identify sections of particular interest to them; they also facilitate later reference to important points. When skillfully used, headings can clarify the organizational scheme of a presentation, let readers see which topics are subordinate to others, and highlight important topics or points of discussion.

David Ewing, in *Writing for Results,* identifies two

types of headings—topical and instructive. A topical heading tells a reader what subject will be discussed beneath it and nothing more. "Market Analysis" is a topical heading. Instructive headings do more than identify a topic: they communicate a theme or point. "Mass Merchandisers to Dominate Market of the 80s" and "Demographic Shifts Mean Shrinking Market for Gizmos" are instructive headings.

Instructive headings usually give more information than topical headings. They also highlight main points. A good set of instructive headings can often be read as a summary of a memo or report. But you should formulate instructive headings with care. Don't make them sound like headlines from the *New York Post.*

Whichever kind of headings you use, try to make them accurate and helpful. Make them truly reflect the discussion they introduce; under "Objectives," don't discuss six other topics. And make them do as much work as possible. Use them to help make transitions, to emphasize points, to interest the reader in the discussion to follow.

Three problems often accompany the use of headings. First, inaccurate headings may be useless or misleading. Overuse of headings and subheadings is another problem commonly found in memos. A complex scheme of headings and subheadings may hinder the reader's understanding of your organizational plan. Also, too many headings can turn a report or memo into a series of fragments. Finally, even when writers use an appropriate number of headings, they may wind up with a bundle of minireports instead of a single cohesive report (or memo) in which each section is logically and clearly related to the next. A heading isn't a substitute for a logical connection, and reports shouldn't be composed from heading to heading like filling in blanks.

You can usually avoid these problems by making headings the last thing you put in your report or memo. Once you have a working draft, you can reasonably assess where headings would be most useful and what they should say.

Lists

Lists enable writers to summarize points economically and set off important points from the body of a paper. Lists provide readers with a change of pace in reading and a break from lines of type.

Unless your list is short, make it vertical to facilitate your reader's grasp of each individual point. Lists in paragraph form are horrible to read. Also, don't make your paper a collection of lists in any form. A bunch of lists isn't compelling reading either.

As you list items, bear in mind the limitations of lists. A list can't communicate relationships between listed points very well. Nor can a list alone convey the relative importance of the listed items. To avoid problems with lists, use them when:

> Summarizing points you've already made or on which you intend to elaborate.
>
> Making points or identifying items similar in nature and importance.
>
> Communicating simple information, like the contents of a shipment.

When you decide to use a list, phrase each point similarly. If you begin one item with a noun, begin the rest with nouns. Don't mix sentences and fragments.

Good	Not so good
1. Increase sales	1. We want increased sales
2. Regroup the marketing department	2. Marketing department—regroup
3. Advertise in magazines	3. Magazine advertising

Indenting, Underlining, and Capitalizing

There devices can help you communicate the structure of your report or memo, emphasize important points, highlight examples, and indicate the relative importance of sections in your report.

Style Applied to the Visual Communication of Information: Graphics in Business Writing

Well-designed tables, charts, diagrams, pictures, and maps allow writers to present information more efficiently, memorably, and accurately than words alone. Poorly designed graphics, however, annoy readers, obscure information, and waste resources.

To use graphics effectively you must:

> Know what and how much information your readers require, and determine when graphic presentation will convey this information more effectively than words alone.
>
> Select an appropriate form of graphic presentation.
>
> Decide how to use the graphics with the text.

WHAT AND HOW MUCH INFORMATION

Some business writers assume the more information they give readers, the better. This is a dangerous assumption, especially in an age when databases and information-retrieval systems abound; keeping informed of new sources of information has become a formidable task in itself. Business writers should present information only to help readers make decisions. Useful information properly presented will answer one of two questions:

> What's happening?
> and
> What may happen in the future?

When writers present information without a clear purpose, they often wind up presenting too much information and forcing readers to sift through pages of facts, tables, statistics, and diagrams that are irrelevant to the issues and decisions at hand. In addition to wasting readers' time, unnecessary information obscures useful information: the truly important facts or statistics become indistinguishable from the mass of irrelevant information.

Even helpful information can be hard to use if its usefulness isn't apparent. When writers know why they're presenting information—when they have a purpose clearly in mind—they're more apt to present the information in ways that will help readers understand, retain, and apply it.

Having determined *what* information to present and *why,* the writer must decide *how* to present it. Graphic forms of presentation—pictures, maps, diagrams, tables, and charts—should be used only when they will help readers grasp information more quickly, understand it better, or recall it more readily than prose alone.

SELECTING AN APPROPRIATE FORM

To determine what kind of graphic to use, the writer must be familiar with the forms of graphic presentation available and understand which forms are best suited to which purposes. Information can be *shown* in a variety of ways: through pictures, maps, diagrams, tables, and charts.

PICTURES

Photographs and drawings can convey a vast amount of detailed information quickly in a relatively small space. They can enliven, clarify, and illustrate prose descriptions of objects, people, or spatial arrangements. However, their strength, economical and accurate depiction of detailed information, can become a weakness if the writer doesn't select, crop, and caption pictures carefully. The wealth of information recorded in photographs can overwhelm viewers and deflect their attention from the point the picture is meant to illustrate.

For example, a report may include photographs to show that certain arrangements of furniture can increase the feeling of spaciousness in an office. But, in addition to showing the pieces of furniture and the spatial relationships among them, the pictures will reveal the posters on the wall, items on the desk, and whether the office is neat, clean, well maintained. The writer, who knows what the picture is meant to illustrate, may not have difficulty extracting information about furniture placement from the mass of other details in the picture. The reader, however, may focus on entirely different information—perhaps on the overflowing wastebasket or the family photos on the desk—and miss the point the writer wished to make.

When selecting pictures, look for ones that emphasize the elements on which you want the reader to concentrate. Cropping (using only a portion of a picture) can also help direct the reader's attention by eliminating unnecessary and distracting details. Captioning—verbally stating the point illustrated in a picture—is one of the most important aspects of picture use. A good caption will both direct attention to the important information in a picture and tell the reader what to conclude from it.

MAPS

Generally, maps show where things are in relation to identifiable landmarks or coordinates. A map can show the boundaries and relative size of a region or the distances between locations more quickly and memorably than can a prose description.

Statistical maps are particularly useful for showing how populations (e.g., catsup consumers, felons, Protestants), events (e.g., catsup purchases, felonies, church attendance), or resources (e.g., tomatoes, jails, churches) are distributed within a geographical region. In such maps, variations in shading, cross-hatching, color, or symbols correspond to variations in the density of populations and resources or the frequency of events.

When designing maps, be sure to provide enough information to situate your reader. Well-known landmarks such as the Statue of Liberty or a large city are often helpful in this respect and may be shown on a map even though not directly related to your main point. Take care, however, to limit yourself to truly helpful or important information. Don't include every local, state, and federal highway on a map designed to show the relative sizes of two sales regions. Unnecessary information only distracts or frustrates readers: resist the temptation to be thorough, if thoroughness accomplishes nothing.

DIAGRAMS

Use these to show the steps in a process or depict relationships. An organizational tree, for example, can show reporting relationships among managers.

Diagrams often illustrate processes or relationships in a highly abstract form; therefore, writers should be careful to ensure that the reader will understand the relationship between the abstract representation and reality. A diagram should simplify processes or relationships to highlight essential features for the reader. Diagrams can become annoyingly complicated when writers try to pack too much information into each one. Once again, if you have a clear sense of what information you need to convey and why, you can usually avoid the pitfall of creating complex diagrams crammed with useless information.

TABLES

These present information in a grid. They are most suitable when readers want access to exact figures or want data in the raw.

Tables are the least graphic way to convey information, short of prose; tables actually communicate very little visually. At best they display how the writer has categorized information (e.g., in terms of sales revenues and years or in terms of units produced per day and absenteeism). They do not effectively *show* the *relationships* between the categories of information tabulated (e.g., that during the past decade revenues have increased, decreased, remained relatively constant, or fluctuated wildly). Tables are wonderful repositories for "background information." However, business writers should be wary of the impulse to provide "background information," which is usually a euphemism for irrelevant or unprocessed facts and data.

When writers understand the significance of information they present and know their purpose for using it in a report, they will often find that charts suit their needs better than tables.

CHARTS

Charts come in many forms. Most of them are variations of five basic types: pie charts, bar charts, column charts, line charts, and surface charts. As noted above, most data that appear in tables can be presented in one or more of these basic chart forms. Which type of chart is most appropriate depends on both the nature of the data and the writer's purpose; different chart forms are effective for showing different comparisons and relationships.

Pie charts show the relative sizes of components that make up a whole (i.e., 100%) and are useful in showing how much each of several parts contributes to a total. They are most effective when the number of components is relatively small (six or fewer is a good rule of thumb) and the components differ significantly in size. Usually, the component you wish to emphasize should be positioned at 12 o'clock.

PIE CHART

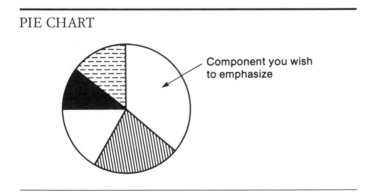

Component you wish to emphasize

Bar charts show the relative sizes or amounts of several items at a given time by means of horizontal bars.

They allow readers to compare magnitudes quickly by sight. Subdivided bars can be used to show how separate components contribute to the total size or amount represented by a single bar.

SIMPLE BAR CHART

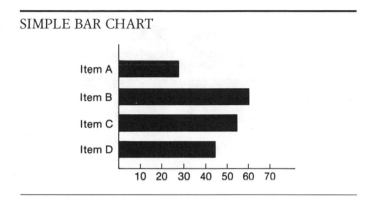

SUBDIVIDED BAR CHART

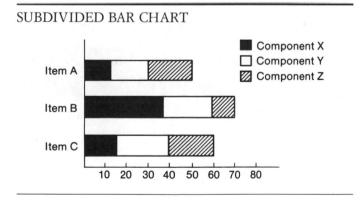

Paired bar charts show co-relationships; for example, a paired bar chart might be used to demonstrate that special point-of-purchase promotions yield significant increases in units sold.

PAIRED BAR CHART

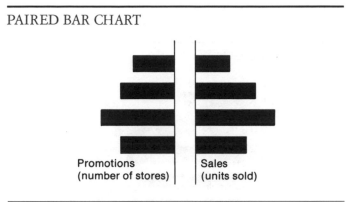

Promotions
(number of stores)

Sales
(units sold)

The most important point to remember about bar charts is that they are *not* used to depict differences in the magnitude of an item at different times; this kind of comparison is generally shown with a column chart or a line chart.

Column charts use vertical columns (rather than horizontal, as in bar charts), and "time" usually appears on the horizontal axis. They show the magnitude of a variable at discrete intervals. Like bars, columns may be subdivided to show how each of several components contributes to a total.

SIMPLE COLUMN CHART

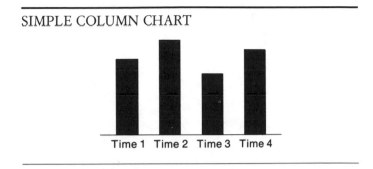

SUBDIVIDED COLUMN CHART

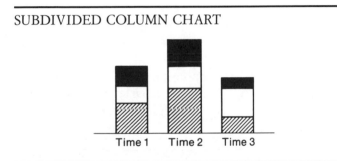

Line charts are most frequently used to show continuous change of a variable over time, although any two variables may be plotted against each other. Line charts often show more than one curve. For example, one line chart may contain several curves representing the unit sales of competing products over the same interval. Writers should, however, limit the number of curves on a single line chart to three or four.

LINE CHART WITH SEVERAL CURVES

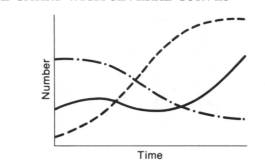

Surface charts are variations on the basic line chart; in fact, the simplest form of a surface chart is a line chart with the area between the curve and the baseline colored or shaded to emphasize the volume under the curve. More complex surface charts, in which areas between two or more curves are shaded, should be used

SIMPLE SURFACE CHART

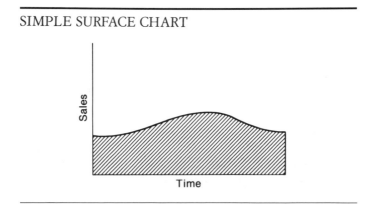

SURFACE CHART SHOWING CONTRIBUTION OF
THREE COMPONENTS TO A TOTAL (100%) OVER
TIME

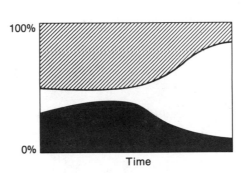

when writers wish to emphasize the distance between
points on two curves rather than the distance between
each curve and the base line. Surface charts are particularly helpful when writers wish to demonstrate how
components change relative to a total over time.

To choose among the five basic chart types, the
writer must become familiar enough with the data and
information to identify a message. A message should
take the form of a statement:

Personnel represents the largest share of Division
A's budget.

Hourly unit production has increased steadily over
the past six months.

There is no correlation between GMAT scores and
grade-point averages among MBAs.

Revenues Projected to Double Next Year.

Note that "messages" take the form of sentences—
they are statements or assertions about the condition of
the world (they answer the questions What's happening? and What may happen?). The following are *not*
statements:

Sales figures for the past 6 months,
Breakdown of Division A's budget,
GMAT Scores and Grades of MBAs,
Sales Projections for next year.

These phrases *name* things but say nothing about the
items named; they neither assert nor state and do not
answer the question What's happening? or the question
What may happen? If you can't make a statement or
assertion about the information before you, you haven't
yet found your message and aren't ready to present the
information to readers.

Facts never speak for themselves, and messages are
often difficult to extract from facts and data. Thus,
experimenting with various chart forms—plotting data
on different kinds of charts—can reveal messages as
well as help writers select the most effective format for
presenting information.

Once a message has been identified, picking the
best chart form becomes relatively easy.

To show how components contribute to a total, use:

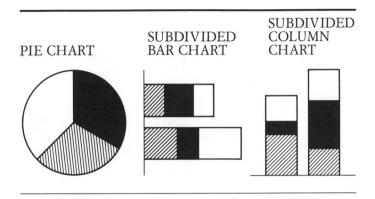

To show how a number of items compare in rank, use:

BAR CHART

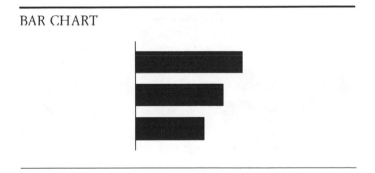

To show how a variable changes over time, use:

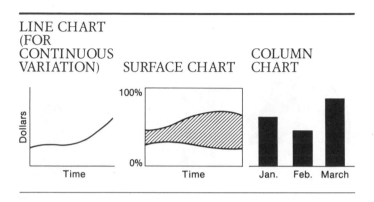

LINE CHART
(FOR
CONTINUOUS   COLUMN
VARIATION)   SURFACE CHART   CHART

To show how two variables are co-related, use:

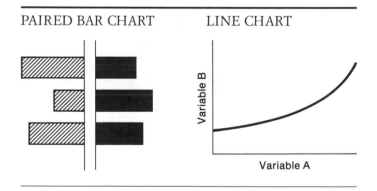

PAIRED BAR CHART   LINE CHART

The five basic chart types can be combined and varied in an infinite number of ways. If you know your message, you can generally design a chart to communicate it clearly, economically, and forcefully.

DESIGNING GRAPHICS

After selecting an appropriate form of graphic presentation for given data, the writer must design the actual chart, table, diagram, or map. A few basic guidelines should inform this process.

First, graphics should always bear titles, and their titles should be clear and informative. The title should usually convey the main message of the graphic. "GMAT Scores Fail to Predict Academic Performance" is a better title than "GMAT Scores and Grades of Currently Enrolled MBAs." The latter title names the information presented but doesn't deliver any message or make any point about it.

Second, all axes, units, scales, symbols, columns, lines, and so forth should be labeled. If different colors, shadings, or symbols have specific meanings, these should be clearly defined in a legend as well.

Third, writers should adhere to the conventional use of the X- and Y-axes. Time usually appears on the X-axis, while money generally appears on the Y-axis. When percent is one of the variables, it is usually plotted on the Y-axis.

Fourth, writers should keep graphics as simple as possible. Exclude extraneous information and limit the number of variables. Avoid the all-purpose chart, table, or diagram that purports to summarize the information and conclusions from 25 pages of text and illustrations. Graphics should simplify, not complicate.

USING GRAPHICS WITH THE TEXT

Now that you've created an effective graphic, do you put it in the text or at the end? And what do you say about it in the text?

Many organizations specify the placement of graphics. Some require all graphics to appear at the end of reports; others demand integration within the text. Frequently, however, the choice is left to the writer.

Graphics placed within the body of a report are more convenient for readers and have a greater impact than graphics placed at the end. Readers are far more likely to examine a table or chart when it's right in front of them. On the other hand, frequent interruptions of the text can become annoying. Also, the temptation to rely too heavily on graphics—to transform the text into a running commentary on the illustrations—increases when graphics and narrative are interwoven. By following a few rules, however, writers can avoid the pitfalls and exploit the advantages of both methods of placing graphic material.

Rule 1. Important information and conclusions contained in illustrations should be stated in the text, regardless of where the graphic is located. In other words, the text should generally be able to stand alone.

Let's suppose Exhibit 1 (shown on page 89) appears in a report recommending the addition of a full-time instructor to the finance faculty at the Well-Known Graduate School of Business.

Let's also suppose that the writer wishes to emphasize the high demand for courses in finance and uses the chart to show that more currently enrolled MBAs major in finance than in any other field. Our writer should state this point clearly in the text. For example:

Finance is the most popular major among today's MBA candidates; 37% of our currently enrolled MBAs list finance as their major or intended major (see Exhibit 1 for a breakdown by major of Well-Known's population).

EXHIBIT 1
FINANCE: THE MOST POPULAR MAJOR

Breakdown of Currently Enrolled MBAs
by Major

Regardless of whether the chart appears in the text or at the end of the report, the writer should state the major point in the narrative. Don't assume that readers will consult the chart or that, if they do, they will draw the desired conclusion or focus on the most relevant information.

Writers should avoid uninformative textual references to graphics:

> Exhibit 1 shows the breakdown of the current MBA population by major. The popularity of finance among MBAs stems from . . . .

This reference fails to state the main point the writer wishes to make about the information portrayed in the chart: more MBAs major in finance than in any other subject. A reader looking at the chart can take much information from it. For instance:

- Fifteen percent of MBAs major in accounting.
- The portion of MBAs majoring in marketing almost equals the portion majoring in finance.
- Twelve percent of MBAs major in operations and production.

A reader may also draw a number of different conclusions from the information. Depending on personal biases, interests, and background, a reader might conclude that:

- Marketing is a surprisingly popular major.
- Relatively few MBAs major in operations.
- Fewer MBAs than expected (by the reader!) major in accounting.

The writer must be careful to direct the reader's attention to the most salient information and clearly state the conclusion(s) to be drawn from it.

Rule 2. In most written reports, the text, not the graphics, should occupy center stage and command the reader's attention. Avoid using the text primarily to talk about the graphics; a well-conceived and well-designed graphic shouldn't require extensive explanation. Major conclusions, assertions, and information conveyed through the graphic should appear in the text (Rule 1), but elaborate descriptions and explanations of the graphic itself should be unnecessary.

Rule 3. Do not include graphics that you don't cite explicitly in the text. Many business reports contain pages and pages of tables, graphs, maps, and diagrams that are never referred to in the text. Such graphics represent wasted time, money, and energy. Few readers will bother to consult graphics not mentioned in the text. Why should they? If the writer doesn't find the information and conclusions in graphics worth mentioning, the reader has little motivation to consult them.

Rule 4. Label graphics, as well as titling them, for ease and accuracy of reference. Citing a chart's or table's full title in the text is often cumbersome, and if you've stated main points from the graphic in your narrative, the full title is often redundant. If you label each graphic (e.g., "Exhibit 1"), you can cite specific graphics quickly and unambiguously in your text (e.g., ". . . see Exhibit 1 for a breakdown of . . .").

Rule 5. When you cite graphics in your narrative, give readers enough information about what they will find when they refer to the graphics to motivate their interest. Don't write merely:

The costs of running the Widget Division have increased sharply in the past year (see Exhibit 1).

Tell your reader what Exhibit 1 (or Table 2 or Figure 8) has to offer. Write:

> The costs of running the Widget Division have increased sharply in the past year (see Exhibit 1 for a breakdown of the Division's annual expenses by line item).

Or write:

> The costs of . . . in the past year (see Exhibit 1 for a breakdown of annual expenses by month).

Notice that the exhibits referenced in the last two examples give different information—provide details about different aspects of the Widget Division's expenses. Readers can't read the writer's mind; they have access only to the writer's words and can't foresee what a graphic will contain. Readers appreciate knowing what a graphic contains so they can decide whether to consult it immediately, come back to it later, or disregard it.

Readers like graphics. Studies indicate that readers respond more favorably to reports with tables and charts than to reports without them. Thus, graphics can secure a warmer reception for your prose. Well-designed graphics can also make important information and conclusions more memorable.

Appendix 1

An Annotated Bibliography for Business Writers

REFERENCES

BERNSTEIN, THEODORE. *The Careful Writer.* New York: Atheneum, 1982. (Available in paperback.)

A standard reference on usage. This or another manual of usage should be available to every writer. Invaluable for determining the correct usage of tricky words like stationary/ stationery, which/that, affect/effect, use/utilize.

BRUSAW, C. T.; ALRED, G. J.; and OLIU, W. E. *The Business Writer's Handbook.* 2d ed. New York: St. Martin's Press, 1982. (Available in paperback.)

An excellent reference book for any writer, not just the business writer. Entries are arranged alphabetically and are thoroughly indexed and cross-indexed, making the book easy to use. The volume covers a remarkable variety of material, ranging from usage problems to designing charts, and contains a minimum of grammatical jargon.

THE EDITORIAL STAFF OF THE UNIVERSITY OF CHICAGO PRESS. *The Chicago Manual of Style.* 13th ed. Chicago: University of Chicago Press, 1982. (Hardcover.)

The final word on questions of punctuation and the mechanics of preparing manuscripts for printing. A bible for professional editors and a good reference for any office. Great for finding answers to those nagging, little, obscure questions that come up now and again and perfect for settling disputes. For example, should you or shouldn't you place a comma between the final elements of a list? Only *The Chicago Manual* knows for sure! (The answer is yes.)

EWING, DAVID. *Writing for Results.* 2d ed. New York: John Wiley & Sons, 1979. (Hardcover.)

This book is actually a text rather than a reference, but it contains much useful advice from a seasoned pro. As Executive Editor of the *Harvard Business Review* and author of many articles and books on business topics, David Ewing knows business prose at its best and its worst. In *Writing for*

Results, he shares his wisdom along with a refreshing dose of wit and many fascinating examples of writing from the real world.

STYLE FOR BUSINESS WRITERS

LANHAM, RICHARD. *Revising Business Prose.* New York: Charles Scribner's Sons, 1981. (Available in paperback.)

Lanham characterizes "official prose," identifies its weaknesses, and suggests methods of revision. A short, enjoyable book but limited in scope. Lanham has written another book, entitled simply, *Revising Prose,* that covers the same material but uses examples drawn from students' themes and academic writing rather than from the business world. Read either one.

SAFIRE, WILLIAM. *William Safire on Language.* New York: Avon, 1980. (Available in paperback.)

For the aficionado and aficionada: a collection of Safire's pieces from the *New York Times Magazine,* including responses from readers. Some of the essays concern fine points that only a dedicated grammar addict could appreciate. Others contain important insights on language, its evolution, and its use as a political tool. All are witty and well written.

STRUNK, WILLIAM, and WHITE, E. B. *The Elements of Style.* 2d ed. New York: Macmillan, 1972. (Available in paperback.)

A classic, and only 75 pages long.

ZINSSER, WILLIAM. *On Writing Well.* New York: Harper & Row, 1976.

This book is aimed at the professional writer of nonfiction but contains advice useful to the business writer as well. Particularly helpful are Zinsser's suggestions for achieving freshness and strength, qualities generally undervalued in business prose.

THE PROCESS OF WRITING

ELBOW, PETER. *Writing with Power.* New York and Oxford: Oxford University Press, 1981. (Available in paperback.)

The "power" in the title refers largely to self-control. Elbow focuses on the processes of writing and thinking; he talks about all kinds of writing, including poetry.

HOLCOMBE, M., and STEIN, J. *Writing for Decision Makers.* Belmont, Calif.: Lifetime Learning Publications, 1981. (Hardcover.)

A readable, straightforward book; especially helpful on organization and structure.

MACK, KARIM, and SKJEI, ERIC. *Overcoming Writing Blocks.* Los Angeles: J. P. Tarcher, 1979. (Available in paperback.)

Like Elbow, these authors concentrate on the process of writing; they offer suggestions for getting started and keeping going.

ZINSSER, WILLIAM. *Writing with a Word Processor.* New York: Harper & Row, 1983.

Zinsser begins with the remark that he's probably one of the last people who'd be expected to compose on a word processor. If you feel the same but have lately begun to question your resistance, you'll enjoy this book. You may even find yourself inspired to experiment.

VIEWS OF COMMUNICATION IN BUSINESS

BURDEN, CHARLES, et al. *Business in Literature.* New York and London: Longmans, 1980. (Available in paperback.)

An anthology of fiction, poems, and essays about working in

business organizations. The editors include many points of view. A sampling from the Table of Contents:

"The Corporation as a Creative Environment" (essay)
"Office Love" (poem)
"Business Values and Artistic Careers" (essays)
"The Computer's First Christmas Card" (poem)
"The Man Higher Up" (short story)
"The Inhumane Businessman" (essay)

Some of the authors: Nietzsche, Zola, Rod McKuen, Peter Drucker, J. Bronowski, Thoreau, e.e. cummings, Jesus.

KANTER, ROSABETH, and STEIN, BARRY. *Life in Organizations.* New York: Basic Books, 1979.

Kanter and Stein have compiled a variety of writings on organizational life as seen from the top, middle, and bottom. They've dedicated their book to:

All of Us Who Live
a Significant Part of Our Lives
in Organizations.

Most of the articles are short and can be read during odd moments. Open it at random now and then.

FOR SPECIAL NEEDS AND INTERESTS

BLY, ROBERT W., and BLAKE, GARY. *Technical Writing: Structure, Standards, and Style.* New York: McGraw-Hill, 1982. (Available in paperback.)

A good book for those coming from engineering backgrounds or going into high-technology companies.

GOLDFARB, RONALD, and RAYMOND, JAMES. *Clear Understandings.* New York: Random House, 1982. (Available in paperback.)

A guide to legal writing, helpful for both writers and readers of legal documents. Legal writing *can* be precise without being obscure!

MACLIN, ALICE. *Reference Guide to English: A Handbook of English as a Second Language.* New York: Holt, Rinehart & Winston, 1981. (Available in paperback.)

A succinct, conveniently indexed reference that includes topics of particular interest to the non-native user of English; e.g., the use of articles (a, an, the). Contains notes on both English and American usage.

Appendix 2

Glossary of Grammatical Terms

Active Voice. (See Voice.)

Adjective. A word or group of words that describes or limits a noun or pronoun.

Adverb. A word or group of words that modifies a verb, adjective, or another adverb.

Antecedent. The noun to which a pronoun refers.

Appositive. A noun (or words used as a noun, such as infinitive phrases, gerunds, pronouns, or noun clauses) that immediately follows another noun and refers to the same person or thing.

Examples: Joann Chapin, *an authority on corporate communications,* addressed senior management.

The new technology, *a great advance over the old,* was warmly received.

Buzzword. An abstract or technical word that has become trendy. Buzzwords sound pretentious while saying very little.

Examples: optimize
minimize
maximize
synergy

Clause. Any group of words with a subject and a verb. A *dependent clause* cannot stand as a complete sentence by itself; it begins with a relative pronoun (*who, which,* or *that*) or subordinating conjunction (*after, as, because, since, when, where, while*).

An *independent clause* can stand as a complete sentence by itself, as distinct from a dependent clause.

Connectives. Words that help tie sentences and thoughts together, such as: and, but, therefore, however, furthermore, on the other hand.

Coordinating Conjunction. A word that joins sentence elements of equal grammatical rank. They are: *and, but, or, nor, for,* and sometimes *yet, so.*

Dependent Clause. (See Clause.)

Expletive. *There* and *it* are expletives when they occur as the subject of a clause but have no denotative meaning.

Examples: *It* is a beautiful day.

There are three barriers preventing us from entering this market.

Independent Clause. (See Clause.)

Jargon. The technical terminology, often idiosyncratic, that characterizes a particular activity or group.'

Modifier. A word, phrase, or clause used to describe, limit, interpret, or change the meaning of another word, phrase, or clause.

Noun. A word that names a person, place, thing, or quality.

Parenthetic Expression. An "unnecessary" interruption in a sentence: something you might enclose in parentheses. A parenthetic expression can be removed from the sentence in which it occurs without a change in meaning.

Example: The industry report, which we received yesterday, presents an optimistic outlook.

Passive Voice. (See Voice.)

Phrase. A group of words that doesn't have a subject and verb and functions as a single part of speech.

Predicate. The verb, its modifiers, and any complements or objects.

Prepositional Phrase. A phrase made up of a preposition, its object, and modifiers of the object.

Examples: We reviewed this portion *of the report* carefully before sending it *to the Vice President of the Northeastern Division.*

Referent. Something referred to.

Subject. The subject is one of the two basic components of a sentence or clause. The other component is the predicate. The subject is the person or thing about which a predicate makes an assertion, asks a question, or gives an order.

Subordinators. Words that connect dependent clauses to independent clauses, placing the two in proper relation to each other. Some subordinators are: *because, before, if, since, which, that,* and *unless.*

Topic Sentence. A topic sentence may occur anywhere in a paragraph, but usually it appears at the beginning and tells the reader what the paragraph is about. A good way to think of a topic sentence is as the most important statement that can be made about the rest of the material in the same paragraph.

Verb. A word that expresses action or a state of being.

Verbiage. Words that serve no purpose other than lengthening a passage: unnecessary words.

Voice. Voice refers to the relationship between the subject and the verb in a sentence or clause. In *active voice,* the subject performs the action designated by the verb. In *passive voice,* the subject receives the action designated by the verb.

Examples: Joseph called Mary. (active)
Mary was called by Joseph. (passive)

Writer's Block. The state of a writer staring blankly out the window with more wishes than words coming to mind.